THE
WORLD
IN YOUR
LUNCH
BOX

THE WORLD IN YOUR LUNCH BOX

Claire Eamer

artwork by
Sa Boothroyd

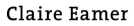

annick press
toronto + new york + vancouver

To Alan and Patrick, my food guys—C.E.
To Mum and Dad—S.B.

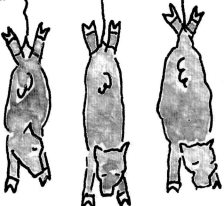

© 2012 Claire Eamer (text)
© 2012 Sa Boothroyd (illustrations)
Third printing, September 2013

Edited by Catherine Marjoribanks
Copyedited by Pam Robertson
Proofread by Elizabeth McLean
Designed by Natalie Olsen, Kisscut Design

Annick Press Ltd.

We acknowledge the support of the Canada Council for the Arts, the Ontario Arts Council, and the Government of Canada through the Canada Book Fund (CBF) for our publishing activities.

ONTARIO ARTS COUNCIL
CONSEIL DES ARTS DE L'ONTARIO

Cataloging in Publication

Eamer, Claire, 1947–

The world in your lunch box : the wacky history and weird science of everyday foods / Claire Eamer ; artwork by Sa Boothroyd.

Includes index.
ISBN 978-1-55451-393-2 (bound).—ISBN 978-1-55451-392-5 (pbk.)

1. Food—Juvenile literature. I. Boothroyd, Sa II. Title.

TX355.E12 2012   j641.3   C2011-907219-X

Distributed in Canada by:
Firefly Books Ltd.
50 Staples Avenue, Unit 1
Richmond Hill, ON
L4B 0A7

Published in the U.S.A. by Annick Press (U.S.) Ltd.
Distributed in the U.S.A. by:
Firefly Books (U.S.) Inc.
P.O. Box 1338   Ellicott Station
Buffalo, NY 14205

Printed in China

Visit us at: www.annickpress.com
Visit Claire Eamer at: www.claireeamer.com
Visit Sa Boothroyd at: www.saboothroyd.com

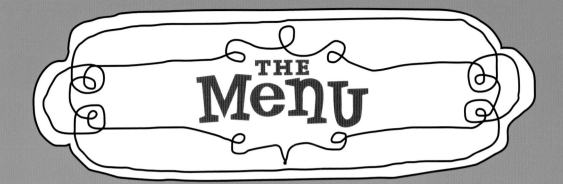

THE Menu

THE LUNCH BOX MISSION

We're learning about cooking this year at school and I thought it would be pretty boring. The cooking teacher says

Boring? NO WAY!

He says everything's interesting if you take the time to learn about it, even stuff as dull as white bread or potatoes. We all groaned when he said that—well, wouldn't you?—but he says he's going to prove it, and we're going to help.

A LUNCH DiaRY

Is your lunch dull, blah, boring?

Have you seen and tasted it all before? Well, don't give up on that sandwich yet! There might be a lot more to it than you realize.

Food doesn't have to be fancy to be interesting. Every kind of food, no matter how basic, has ties with exciting history, amazing science, and some very strange stories. One kind of food travels halfway around the world to reach you; another comes from just down the road. Your favorite sandwich was soldier's rations centuries ago. Your favorite fruit could come from a desert in Africa, and your favorite vegetable from a mountainside in Peru.

Wars have been fought over food. People have been killed by food or for food. Others have been saved by it. Some foods are created by complicated chemical reactions. Others create chemical reactions when you eat them.

Your job is to keep a lunch diary that tracks your lunch for a whole week. Then we'll do some research and see where it takes us. I'm guessing we'll find prehistoric nomads, ancient tombs, explorers' ships, maybe even a little mad science.

eXtReMe FooD:

THE BISHOP WHO ATE HIS BOOTS

In 1909, Bishop Isaac Stringer and a companion set out to travel 800 kilometers (500 miles) through Canada's far north. They were used to the wilderness and figured they could reach Dawson City in the Yukon in five days. But they hit bad weather and worse luck— and spent 51 days slogging through fresh snow, fog, and freezing cold. Near the end, they even ran out of food. The only thing left was their boots, made of sealskin with walrus-hide soles. They cut the boots into pieces, boiled them for hours, and then roasted them. For the last four days of the journey, just before they were rescued, they ate nothing but boots toasted over the fire. The soles, Bishop Stringer wrote, tasted better than the tops.

SEAL BOOT SOUP

4

DAY 1 MONDAY

My lunch diary: This is the first day of my lunch diary, and my lunch is pretty dull, mostly leftovers from the weekend. A ham sandwich, with slices of last night's supper ham on white bread. Cherry tomatoes, from my aunt's garden. Chunks of the watermelon we brought to Saturday's picnic. Not much excitement there.

Don't judge too soon... This lunch might be more interesting than you think. I want you to investigate HAM, BREAD, TOMATOES, AND WATERMELON.

Good luck!

MY LUNCH DIARY

Dear Diary,

Today I ate lunch. It was pretty boring but Kaitlyn traded me her granola bar for my cherry tomatoes. She is a tomato freak.

this is Kaitlyn →

The arm of the Earl of Sandwich

bread wrapper

cooked beef

beef grease

How much the Earl ate in 24 hours of gambling

meat slices

fresh bread

How much the Earl won at gambling

The Earl's Lunch

According to an 18th-century travel writer, the sandwich was named for the fourth Earl of Sandwich, who once gambled for 24 hours straight, eating slices of beef stuck between two pieces of bread to keep himself going. He's certainly not the only one in history who used bread as a wrapper for other food, but he's the one whose name stuck.

- [ ] **HAM**
- [ ] BREAD
- [ ] TOMATOES
- [ ] WATERMELON

LUNCH ON THE MARCH

About 1800 years ago, a small group of Roman soldiers stopped for lunch in the shadow of Hadrian's Wall, the great stone barrier that cut across Britain and marked the farthest edge of the Roman Empire. They were patrolling, on the lookout for intruders from the unconquered north. The soldiers built a small fire and dug food and cooking gear out of their packs. Soon, the smell of fried ham drifted over the northern heather. The soldiers smeared their ham with mustard paste from a small pot and cut off hunks from a loaf of heavy bread. Crouching in the fire's warmth, they munched on something pretty close to a ham sandwich.

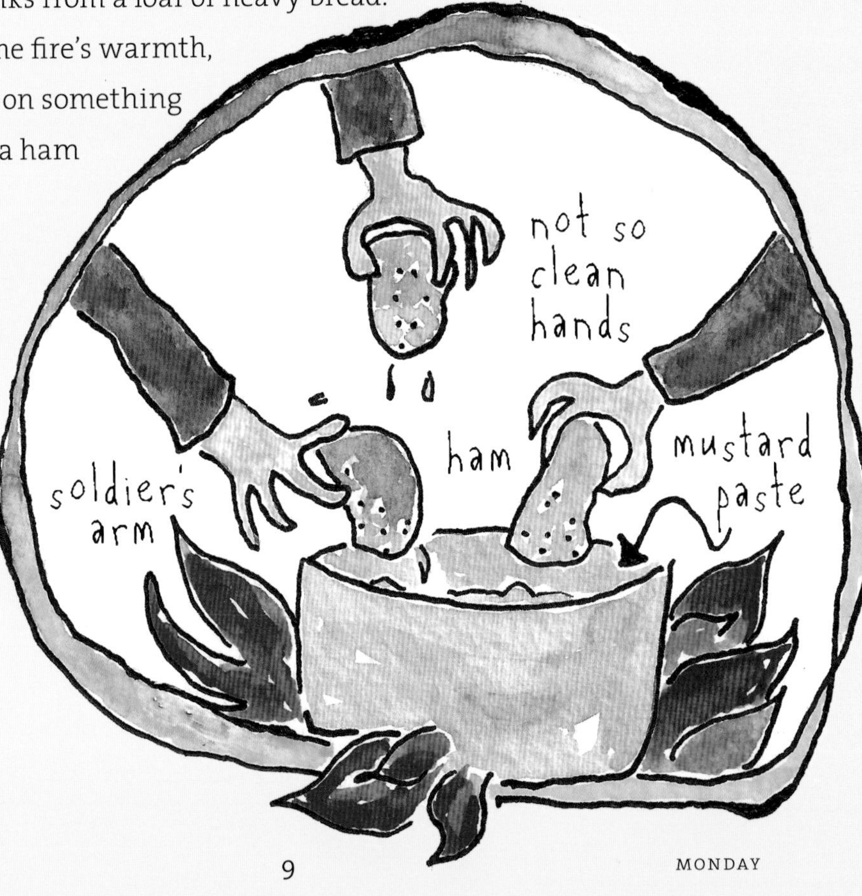

not so clean hands
ham
soldier's arm
mustard paste

HISTORY

The Romans didn't invent ham. They picked up a taste for it—and some good recipes, too—when they conquered the people known as Gauls, who lived in northern France. The Gauls ate lots of meat, especially pork from domestic pigs and wild boar. To make it last longer, they cured it with salt. The largest chunks, usually from the thick part of the leg, were used for ham.

In the Middle Ages in Europe, any family that could afford it kept a pig. In the fall, before the winter made pig feed scarce, they would slaughter the pig, salt the meat, and hang hams from the rafters, safe from rats and mice. All you had to do to check your winter meat supply was look up.

Salt and Smoke

PIG IN SALT FOR 2 WEEKS

Today, we stick meat in the fridge or the freezer

to keep it fresh, but without a fridge it can go bad really fast. Before fridges and freezers were common, salt was the answer. More than 2000 years ago, the Roman writer Cato wrote about how to make ham. Pack large cuts of pork in salt for a couple of weeks, he instructed, and then hang them in the smoke of an open fire for several days. The meat will last weeks or months without spoiling.

That's mainly because of the salt. Microbes, the tiny organisms that make meat spoil, are single cells made mostly of water. Salt attracts water. Just think how thirsty you get when you eat salty chips or popcorn. In ham, the salt sucks the water out of the microbes, killing them before they can spoil the meat. It also affects proteins in meat in much the same way cooking does, so using salt can be a kind of heatless cooking.

Smoking the ham gives it another layer of protection. Smoke contains hundreds of chemical compounds. Some of them kill the microbes on the meat's surface. Others coat the meat in a fine layer that keeps oxygen out, stopping more of the chemical reactions that cause meat to spoil.

SCIENCE

☑ HAM
☐ **BREAD**
☐ TOMATOES
☐ WATERMELON

SHOW ME THE DOUGH!

Bread has really worked its way into our language. "Bread" and "dough" are both slang for money. The word "companion" comes from *companio,* Latin for "one who shares the bread." "Lord" and "lady" come from Anglo-Saxon words that meant "loaf guardian" and "loaf kneader." Bread has clearly been a big deal for a long time.

To make bread, you need grain—and people have been growing grain for more than 9000 years. Then you need ways to grind the grain into flour and bake the bread. A couple of stones and a clay oven will work. The tomb of an Egyptian noblewoman who died almost 5000 years ago contained small loaves of barley bread, and a 3300-year-old Egyptian temple wall has a drawing of a workman eating his lunch—a cucumber, an onion, and a chunk of bread.

Even in ancient Egypt, some bread was considered better than other bread. If you could afford it, you bought wheat flour, which made finer, lighter bread. And the whiter, the better. White bread was a luxury in Greece, Rome, and even medieval Europe. For much of history, in fact, only the wealthy could afford the kind of bread we use today for ordinary lunchtime sandwiches.

made with
wheat flour →

yummy yummy
ancient Egyptian
white bread →

A Medieval Child's Lunch

Poor people in medieval Europe could rarely afford the flour to make bread. Instead they ate pottage, all day and every day. Pottage was a porridge made of sprouted barley grains boiled in a big pot over the fire. The cook would throw in whatever else might be available—maybe dried peas or beans, and a little salt pork if the family could spare it. In summer, onions, garlic, fresh vegetables, wild nuts and roots, or even fruit could be thrown into the pot. In winter, the pottage was probably made of little more than barley. For a peasant child, lunch was a helping of pottage, and supper was more of the same.

Cook having some fun at work

13

BUBBLING UP

The kind of bread we slice up for sandwiches owes its fluffiness to something called a leavening agent. Usually, the agent is yeast. Yeast is a fungus, like mushrooms. When it's dry, yeast looks like powder or tiny pellets smaller than the head of a pin. But when it's wet, the yeast gets busy. When you mix yeast into bread dough, the little yeast cells gobble up sugars in the dough and burp out bubbles of carbon dioxide gas. And the bubbles make the dough puff up, or rise.

The yeast cells gobble and burp as long as the temperature suits them. If they get too cool, their gobbling and burping will slow down to a crawl. Too much heat will kill them and put an end to the process. But if loaves of dough sit in a warm place, away from drafts, the tiny bubbles can puff them up to two or three times their original size in just a couple of hours.

Next, the loaves go into the oven. The heat of the oven kills the yeast cells and cooks off the carbon dioxide in the bubbles. What remain are the bubble holes that give loaves of leavened bread their fluffy texture.

SCIENCE

WOW

Yeast looks like tiny

pellets when it's dry

YEAST

but when it's wet

it gets busy

IS

Little yeast cells gobble

up sugars in the dough

QUITE

then burp out bubbles

of carbon dioxide gas

COOL

DeADLy
RELATIVES

No Roman soldier, Egyptian noblewoman, or medieval farmer ever ate tomatoes, or even knew they existed. Tomatoes come from South America, and their seeds first migrated north to Mexico, probably in the droppings of birds. The Aztecs cultivated the plant and called it *tomatl,* or "plump fruit."

The Spanish conquered the Aztec Empire in the 16th century, and when they carried Aztec gold back to Europe, tomatoes came along for the ride. At first the Europeans didn't know what to do with them. Then, a Spanish priest wrote that the Indians of Central America turned tomatoes into sauce. After that, there was no holding tomatoes back. Within a century, they were on the menu as far away as Nepal.

But not in northern Europe. There, people thought tomatoes were poisonous. After all, tomatoes are related to deadly nightshade, a famous poison blamed for sickening and killing whole armies. Despite its unpleasant relatives, however, the tomato is tasty and harmless. After a couple of centuries, even northern Europeans and North American settlers were convinced and put tomatoes on the table.

HEY, watch out for the bird poop!

But I think there are tomato seeds in there.

HISTORY

MONDAY

BetteR, NOT BitteR

The ancestor of the tomato was a bitter berry growing wild on bushes on the dry west coast of South America. When the seeds of the berry made it north to the Aztecs in Mexico, the farmers planted them, tended them, and chose the biggest and sweetest tomatoes to replant. Over time, they turned a small, bitter berry into a plump, juicy fruit.

After the Spanish took tomatoes back to Europe, plant growers around the world had a chance to do the same thing. Today, tomatoes range from grape-sized to grapefruit-sized and come in a variety of colors, including red, yellow, green, orange, black, and even striped. But they all trace their ancestry back to South American berries about the size of small cherry tomatoes.

LuncH LauGHS

Q: How do you fix a broken tomato?

a: With tomato paste, of course!

SCIENCE

a tReat IN THE Heat

More than 10,000 years ago, in Africa's Kalahari Desert, a family of wanderers might have shared some watermelons for lunch. Those melons would have been much smaller than the ones we know today, and not nearly as sweet. Still, they would have been a welcome source of water in a place with very little.

Over time, wild watermelons from the Kalahari were carried to other parts of the world, cultivated, and made sweeter. We know there were big green watermelons in ancient Egypt, because people painted pictures of them on the walls of buildings. They even left watermelon seeds behind. The seeds might have come from someone's lunch— or perhaps, thousands of years ago, a couple of water boys sat in the shade of a brand-new pyramid and squirted fresh watermelon seeds at each other.

HISTORY

Slave ships carried watermelons to the Americas four centuries ago, and everyone—from European settlers to Native Americans—began growing and eating them. They grew them bigger, too. Some kinds of watermelon grown today can weigh up to 45 kilograms (99 pounds). You'd need a weightlifter to carry that home for supper!

NATURE'S OWN
Water Bottle

Watermelons are more than 90 percent water,
and their rinds keep that water trapped inside the fruit. Eating a slice of watermelon is almost like taking a drink. That makes melons valuable in places where water is scarce and not necessarily safe. People on desert journeys have been known to carry watermelons as a kind of natural canteen.

Watermelons have special adaptations that let them hold and keep water, even in extremely hot, dry places. The melon's thick rind is waxy on the outside. That helps keep its contents from drying out. Inside, watermelon cells are large and bulging with water. In fact, the cells of watermelons are so large that you can often see them with the naked eye. With a magnifying glass, you can see them even more clearly. Examining your chunk of watermelon is a good way to see what plant cells look like.

SCIENCE

19

DAY 2 TUESDAY

My lunch diary: That first lunch was a bit surprising—I didn't expect Roman soldiers! Today, we have cooking class, and we're learning to make one of my favorites: macaroni and cheese. And the best part is, we get to eat it for lunch. Hope it's as good as my grandma's. She makes the best macaroni and cheese ever, with lots of yummy cheese, and a sprinkling of freshly ground pepper. For dessert, we've got seedless green grapes. I hate seeds, so I'm glad, but how can you grow more grapes if you don't have seeds to plant?

I'd like to try your grandmother's macaroni and cheese. Sounds delicious, and pepper would really add something to the flavor. Take a look at MACARONI — it has some strange connections.
Also, find out more about CHEESE, BLACK PEPPER, and, of course, GRAPES.

TUESDAY

☐ **MACARONI**
☐ CHEESE
☐ BLACK PEPPER
☐ GRAPES

National NOODLES

Macaroni is a kind of pasta, or Italian-style, wheat-based noodle. The word "macaroni" comes from *maccheroni*, which was an early word for all kinds of pasta. Today it's just used for short, tube-shaped noodles, one of the first kinds of pasta developed in Italy. In a cookbook from 1420, there's a Sicilian recipe for macaroni that uses flour, eggs, and rosewater, with cheese sprinkled on top, so clearly macaroni and cheese have made a good team for a long time.

Italians are proud of their noodles, but so are the Chinese. In China, noodles are made from rice, beans, and even root vegetables, as well as wheat. And the Chinese have been making noodles for a long time. A few years ago, a scientist turned over an ancient pot buried 3 meters (10 feet) deep in the floodplain of the Yellow River and discovered somebody's long-lost lunch—long, skinny, yellow noodles made from ground millet seeds about 4000 years ago. The pot was probably tipped over and buried in a flood, sealing the noodles inside for all those centuries. After so long, I don't suppose anyone volunteered to try them!

27-year-old arm

4000-year-old noodles

NOTE FROM ILLUSTRATOR: DO NOT EAT A 4000-YR-OLD NOODLE IF YOU FIND ONE. JUST LOOK AT IT AND POKE IT.

☑ MACARONI
☐ CHEESE
☐ BLACK PEPPER
☐ GRAPES

SLIPPING AND SLIDING

When you think about it, noodles are amazing.

They can sit in the cupboard for years, as dry as dust. If you try to bend them, they snap or shatter. But if you cook them in boiling water, they're transformed. They swell up and turn into soft, flexible, tasty tubes or strips—and it's all because of the gluten.

Gluten is a substance in flour. It's made of protein molecules, too small to see without a powerful microscope, that are strung together in long chains. When they're dry, the chains lock stiffly into place and don't bend. If you get the gluten chains wet, though, they start to slip and slide around each other. They can bend and even stretch a bit without breaking. If you've ever seen someone tossing and stretching pizza dough, you've seen gluten at work. It's what lets the dough stretch without tearing. You can do the same thing with noodle dough.

When macaroni noodles are dried for packaging, the gluten loses its water and goes stiff. Yet all it takes to get those gluten chains slipping and sliding again is a few minutes in some nice hot water. Now that's weird science.

I think Mom and Dad are losing it...

Couple testing how far their spaghetti will stretch.

23

AND THE PRiZe goes to...

According to one estimate, there are at least 1500 different kinds of cheeses in the world, and each kind tastes different—to experts, anyway.

Some cheeses are made and eaten on the same day, but most cheeses hang around much longer, getting better and better as they age. The record for the oldest cheese (at least, for a cheese still worth eating) goes to a 200-year-old hard Swiss cheese called Saanen. Even cheddar, the most common hard cheese in the world—and an important part of macaroni and cheese—can be several years old before it gets to the grocery store and into your lunch.

Not sure we'll fit under that bridge...

WISCONSIN CHEDDAR

And the biggest cheese? For more than a century, two English villages held the record with a giant cheese they created for Queen Victoria's wedding in 1840. The monster cheddar measured 2.7 meters (9 feet) across and weighed 567 kilograms (1250 pounds), roughly the weight of a cow. That record stood until 1964, when American cheese makers in Wisconsin made a cheddar that weighed about as much as 27 cows. Imagine the pile of macaroni you'd need to go with that much cheese!

The stinkier the better for Emperor Charlemagne.

Stinky Cheese Rules!

Sometime around the year 800, Emperor Charlemagne of France had dinner with a bishop, who served him cheese covered with mold. Trying to be polite, the emperor cut the mold away and ate the white cheese that remained. "Don't do that, my lord!" the bishop said. "You're throwing away the best part." So Charlemagne screwed up his courage and nibbled a bit of moldy cheese. It was wonderful—so good, in fact, that he ordered the bishop to deliver two cartloads of stinky, moldy cheese to the imperial court every year.

A HAPPY accident

Cheese was almost certainly discovered by accident.
It happened thousands of years ago, probably somewhere east of the
Mediterranean Sea, and it went pretty much like this: Someone poured
the last of the day's milk into a bag made from a calf's stomach. A few
hours later, the milk had spoiled, but in an interesting way. It separated
into watery liquid and crumbly solids. Some hungry person bravely tried
the crumbly bits—and they tasted good! Even better,
they stayed edible longer than the milk stayed fresh.

Thank you, calf.

the first stomach
that made cheese

SCIENCE

The crumbly bits were curds, which are the basic material of cheese. And why were the curds discovered in a bag made from a calf's stomach? That's because calves' stomachs contain rennet, a substance that helps the young animals digest their mother's milk. When it's mixed with curds, rennet makes them softer and tastier.

The watery liquid, called whey, is drained off, but it isn't wasted. Remember Little Miss Muffett, who ate both her curds and her whey? Whey is often turned into protein powder and added to manufactured foods, such as crackers and ice cream, so you might be eating it too, without even knowing it.

Lunch Laughs

Q: What do you call a package of cheddar that isn't yours?

a: Nacho cheese!

A SPICY TREASURE

It might be hard to imagine, but ordinary black pepper was once a treasure so rare that it could make your fortune. The Romans loved pepper so much that they built huge warehouses just to store shipments of it. In the fifth century, an army of barbarians known as the Visigoths besieged Rome. Their leader, Alaric, announced that he'd spare the city if the Romans paid him a huge ransom that included 1360 kilograms (3000 pounds) of black peppercorns. The Romans paid. . . but then Alaric came back a couple of years later and sacked the city anyway.

Gimme all your pepper!

A thousand years after that, Europeans imported black pepper all the way from the coastal mountains of tropical India. Portugal alone sent half a dozen ships to India each year. They were huge ships, like floating warehouses, with two entire decks designed to hold nothing but pepper. It was a long, expensive, and dangerous voyage that went all the way around Africa. Soon the European nations started looking for an easier sea route to India.

And that is how European explorers stumbled on the Americas. They weren't looking for a new continent. They were looking for a faster, cheaper way to get black pepper.

29

Salt for Gold

Like pepper, salt was once a treasure to those who could mine and sell it. In salt mines deep in the Sahara Desert, salt was dug up, carved into blocks, and loaded on hundreds of camels to be carried south to the trading city of Timbuktu. People from saltless lands farther south bought Saharan salt with what their own mines produced—gold. In the 13th century, explorer Marco Polo reported that small blocks of salt were used as money in parts of China. And 14th-century traveler Ibn Battuta wrote about the strange salt-mining town of Taghaza, where the walls of houses and even the mosque were made of salt blocks. If rain ever fell in the dry Sahara, the whole town would have melted away.

BEYOND BASIC BLACK

Farming pepper takes a lot of planning. The hard, dry peppercorns we grind up and sprinkle on our food start out as berries growing in long bunches on a vine. A single stem of a pepper vine can produce as many as 30 bunches of berries, but only when the vine is four to seven years old. To keep a steady supply of pepper, farmers have to keep planting new vines and weeding out the ones that don't produce berries anymore.

Pepper berries are dried to create the peppercorns we buy in stores. Although black pepper is the official name, the peppercorns actually come in white, green, pink, and red, too, depending on when they're picked and how they are processed. Peppercorns can last 10 years without losing their strength. Once you grind up the peppercorns to sprinkle on food, though, they start to lose their zip. Freshly ground pepper has more flavor, no matter how old the peppercorns are.

SCIENCE

Don't forget the pepper!

Sweet Business

Ancient Egypt's boy pharaoh Tutankhamen

must have liked grapes. About 3300 years ago, a mourner left a dish of grapes in his tomb to supply him in the afterlife. The ancient Greeks and Romans loved grapes, too. They ate fresh grapes, made wine with them, and dried them to produce raisins and currants.

Grapes are native to North America, Asia, and southern Africa, too. Almost a thousand years ago, the Greenland Vikings sailed to North America and called the land they found Vinland, for the wild grapevines they found there. Today, no one knows exactly where Vinland was. However, since wild grapes grow only as far north as New Brunswick in Canada, the Viking ships must have sailed at least that far south.

Today, growing grapes, especially for wine, is a huge international industry. Even Australia, with no native grapes of its own, has vineyards full of grape varieties imported from around the world. Many modern varieties are hybrids—crosses between different grapes that might have originated oceans apart. It's even possible that someone, somewhere, has crossed the grapes Tutankhamen ate with Vinland's wild grapes to create an entirely new variety.

HISTORY

When Granny wasn't making macaroni and cheese, she liked to feed Grampa grapes.

PLANTING
WITHOUT SEEDS

"Seedless" grapes actually have seeds, but usually they're so tiny you don't notice them, and they're too underdeveloped to grow into plants. But that doesn't really matter, as grapes aren't usually grown from seed. Commercial grapevines are grown from pieces of stem or root cut from mature grapevines. The cuttings are placed in moist sand and treated with hormones that encourage them to develop roots. Then they can be planted in soil, where they will grow into new plants. The new vines are clones, exact genetic copies of the vine the cuttings came from.

Yippee!

William Thompson and his one surviving grape plant.

SCIENCE

The seedless grapes in our lunches today are likely descendants of a single cutting sent from New York and planted by California grape grower William Thompson almost a century and a half ago. Only a few months after it was planted, winter floods wiped out most of Thompson's grapes. However, the new cutting survived and grew into a mature vine. The descendants of that vine, which became known as the Thompson Seedless grape, now supply most of the seedless green grapes in North American grocery stores, as well as grape juice, wine, and 95 percent of the raisins produced in California.

LUNCH LAUGHS

Q: What did the green grape say to the purple grape?

A: Breathe! Breathe!

DAY 3

WEDNESDAY

My lunch diary: Field trip to the museum today! We're eating in the cafeteria, and there's a huge dinosaur right outside the entrance—just the skeleton, of course. There are lots of bad jokes going around about dino-dogs and dino-burgers. Anyway, I've got lunch money in my pocket and a whole cafeteria to choose from. What does that mean? Junk food! A hot dog, chips, and ice cream.

Yuck! Not the world's healthiest meal, but it's your choice today. Might as well know what you're eating, though. Are you putting mustard on that dog? Maybe you can dig up some information about HOT DOGS, MUSTARD, POTATO CHIPS, AND ICE CREAM.

DOGS IN THE PARK

What do you call the sausage part of a hot dog?

A wiener or a frankfurter? Both might be right. According to people in Frankfurt, Germany, it's called a frankfurter because it's a traditional sausage that Frankfurt butchers have been making since the Middle Ages. But in Vienna, Austria, they say the hot dog sausage is their invention, so it's called a wiener—from Wien (*veen*), the Austrian name for Vienna.

But what about the "dog" bit? Relax! Hot dogs were never made from dogs. Nobody knows for sure where the name came from, but here's the most popular theory. Around 1900, hot dogs were already being sold at baseball games in the United States. They were sometimes called "dachshund sausages" because they were long and tube-shaped, just like the dogs. A popular sports cartoonist named Tad Dorgan drew a cartoon of a man selling hot "dachshund sausages" in buns at the ballpark. He wasn't sure how to spell "hot dachshund" so he wrote "hot dog." And the name stuck.

Don't put me in a bun.

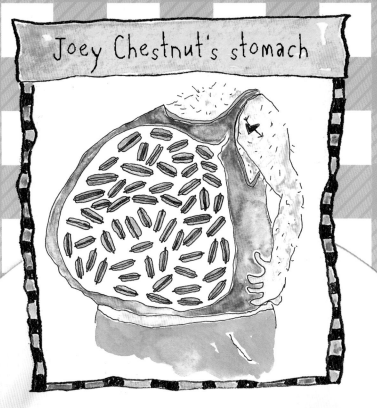

Joey Chestnut's stomach

Too Dog-gone Many!

On July 4, 2009, Joey "Jaws" Chestnut set a world record at the 94th annual Nathan's Hot Dog Eating Contest on Coney Island, New York. The California construction engineer ate 68 hot dogs, buns and all, in 10 minutes. That's roughly 19,000 calories, or enough calories to get at least six men through the day. He even beat legendary competitive eater Takeru "The Tsunami" Kobayashi. Kobayashi, who has appeared in cartoons and commercials, is famous for shattering eating records, while staying slim by exercising—hard!

MysteRy Meat

Hot dogs have never been made from dogs,

but they've had some pretty strange ingredients over the years. Mass-produced hot dogs used to be made from all the bits left over after a pig or a cow was cut up for meat—sometimes including the floor sweepings. Hot dogs are still made from leftover bits of meat, but government regulations mean the floor sweepings are left out.

I wouldn't eat those bits

GOVERNMENT REGULATIONS SAY THESE BITS SHOULD NOT BE IN YOUR HOT DOG. LET'S HOPE THIS PERSON HAS READ THAT DOCUMENT.

Here are a few of the ingredients that might be in your hot dog, besides pork or beef:

> animal fat, to make the sausage juicier and prevent shrinkage when it's cooked

> vegetable oil, to replace a portion of the animal fat with something a bit healthier

> sugar, mainly for flavor

> salt, for flavor and to help preserve the meat

> nitrite, a chemical designed to prevent spoilage

> garlic and various spices, again for flavor

> red food coloring, to keep the sausage the pink-brown color we expect

A GOOD THING GeTS aRouND

The Romans often get the credit for the spread of mustard plants around Europe and Asia. That's because mustard-loving Roman soldiers carried mustard seeds with them to every corner of the empire. To add flavor to their food, they ground mustard seeds to a powder and mixed the powder with a little wine or vinegar. The result was a mustard paste much like the mustard you buy in grocery stores today.

The spread of mustard probably didn't have much to do with the Romans, though. Mustard plants grow so quickly and easily that they could have spread on their own. Mustard seeds have been found in ancient sites from Europe to China, including Egyptian tombs more than 3300 years old. In medieval Europe, mustard was so popular that some courts paid a special official called a *mustardarius* just to oversee mustard production.

Most people think of mustard as food, but it has also been used as medicine. Pythagoras, a mathematician and physician in ancient Greece, recommended mustard to treat scorpion stings. Some people still use mustard plasters to treat colds or rheumatism. You mix powdered mustard and flour with water or egg white, spread the mixture on a soft cloth, and place it on the affected part of the body. But be careful! Straight mustard can burn your skin.

Honest, Dad, it will feel better soon

H2O
FLOUR
mustard

Cutting the Mustard

In 1850s England, most of the dry mustard sold in stores was fake. Arthur Hill Hassall, who led a campaign against fake food, slogged all over London in search of good mustard. He bought 42 samples from 42 different shops, and not a single sample was pure mustard, as advertised. Most were cheap flour, colored bright yellow, with just enough mustard mixed in to fool the customers.

so HOT it HURtS

The yellow mustard that usually comes with hot dogs has a fairly mild flavor, but not all mustards are alike. Have you ever tried really hot mustard? Or a little too much wasabi, the green stuff that comes with sushi? It can make your eyes water, your nose run, and your head feel ready to explode. Mustard and wasabi belong to the cabbage family, and they both contain tiny chemical hotness bombs designed to protect their seeds.

Mustard's hotness chemicals are stored in the seeds' cells. You can't normally taste or smell them because they're protected by a chemical lock. Each hotness molecule is locked to a sugar molecule, and as long as the molecules remain stuck together, the mustard seed just tastes bitter.

SCIENCE

However, if an animal bites off a mouthful of mustard and starts chewing up the seeds, that breaks the lock and sets off the hotness bomb. The damaged cells release a chemical called an enzyme that splits the sugar molecule from the hotness molecule. The hotness molecules turn into fumes that flood the animal's mouth and nose. Suddenly, the animal's nose is burning, its eyes are watering, and it loses interest in eating any more mustard. At least, that's the theory. It's just bad luck for mustard (and wasabi) plants that some people like that sense of burning heat when they eat!

Black mustard seeds make the hottest mustard. Mild hot dog mustard is made from white mustard seeds. How you prepare the mustard matters too. Mixing ground mustard seeds with liquid helps make it hot, but— strange as it sounds— cold liquid makes it hotter. Hot liquid cooks the mustard's heat away, making the mustard taste milder.

A little too much wasabi!

WEDNESDAY

"CHiPS" OR "CRiSPS"?

Talking about potato chips is tricky. In North America, the salty, deep-fried potato slices that come in a package are called "chips." In Britain, they're called "crisps." In New Zealand, the same things are called "cold chips."

Whatever you call them, they've been around longer than you probably realize. Recipes for deep-frying thin slices of raw potato go as far back as 1795 in France and the early 1800s in the United States. Credit for inventing the modern potato chip usually goes to George Crum, a chef in New York State in the early 1850s.

As the story goes, a customer sent back his french fries, complaining they were too thick. Crum was annoyed and decided to teach the customer a lesson. He cut a potato into the thinnest slices he could, deep-fried them quickly, and sent the crisp, oily chips back to the customer. To Crum's amazement, the customer loved them—and other people started asking for them too. When Crum opened his own restaurant a few years later, he placed a basket of potato chips on every table.

Ha! This will teach them

Potato School?

In Britain, your "crisps" come in a bag, but your "chips" might come with fish—they're what North Americans think of as french fries. Of course, in France they are known as pommes frites, *instead. In Canada you can enjoy your potatoes as* poutine, *which means the fries are topped with generous amounts of cheese curds and gravy. In the Netherlands, where fries are known as* patat, *they are served in paper cones with mayonnaise. And do the Belgians ever love their fries! Per capita, there are 11 times as many* frites *stands in Belgium as there are McDonald's outlets in the United States. You can even go to a special school there to learn all the secrets of proper* frites *preparation.*

SCIENCE

IT'S IN tHe BaG

Americans could buy pre-cooked potato chips
as long ago as the 1870s, but chips that come in their own bag,
pre-salted and flavored, weren't invented until the 20th century.

Packaged potato chips stay fresh and crispy for a couple of
months after they're made—and it's all because of the bags. The
bags often have a foil lining or some other coating that keeps light
from reaching the chips, and the gas inside the bag is nitrogen,
not air, which contains oxygen. Both light and oxygen can trigger
chemical processes that would spoil the chips. The bags are also
waterproof, to keep out moisture that would make the chips soggy.

Chips are tasty but they don't offer much real food value.
They're mostly oil and salt, with a little bit of potato to hold it all
together. The flavoring comes from powders that taste like food
without actually containing any healthy ingredients. Delicious, yes.
Nutritious? Well... maybe not!

COLD is HOT!

Ice cream lovers can thank an American,

Nancy Johnson of Philadelphia, for helping bring their favorite dessert into every home. In 1843, she patented the first hand-cranked ice cream maker. Before that, making ice cream was a slow process that required big chunks of ice (no electric fridges and freezers in those days), and lots of stirring and scraping by hand so that ice crystals wouldn't form. And all that work still produced only tiny amounts of the lovely stuff. The new ice cream maker could turn out delicious ice cream much faster.

About 10 years later, Jacob Fussell, a dairy farmer in Baltimore, launched the first ice cream factory, and then opened ice cream parlors across America. Because he could make the product in such large amounts, he was able to sell it at a price most people could afford.

HISTORY

49

Americans were hooked! And they are still among the world's champion ice cream eaters. Americans and Australians ate an average of about 18 liters (4.75 U.S. gallons) of ice cream per person in 2007—that's about 75 bowls. New Zealanders beat them both by just a couple of liters.

Today, ice cream comes in too many flavors to count, but the most popular flavor... care to guess? Yes, it's still vanilla.

A Thorny Solution

Vanilla was once a delicacy reserved for Incan royalty. Why was it so rare? Because vanilla flowers open for only a single day. If they are not pollinated by birds or bees during those few hours, the flowers drop off the vine without producing bean pods. But in 1841, a slave boy on Réunion, an island in the Indian Ocean, solved the problem. Edmond Albius figured out how to hand-pollinate the vanilla orchids on his master's plantation by using a thorn to move a flap in the flower and press the male and female flower parts together. And that's how it's done to this day. Each individual flower has to be pollinated by hand, which is why true vanilla is still one of the most expensive spices in the world.

Birds do it, bees do it...

COLD CHemiStRy

Ice cream making is all about chemistry.

And sometimes, chemistry can be delicious!

If all you do is put cream in the freezer, you don't get ice cream—you just get a dish of rock-hard frozen cream. Adding sugar will sweeten the cream and make it softer when frozen, but it creates a new problem. Cream freezes when its water molecules get cold enough to line up in neat rows that form crystals. However, the sugar molecules in sweetened cream get in the way of the water molecules and make it harder for them to line up. So you need much lower temperatures to freeze cream with sugar added.

If you put your container of sweetened cream into a bucket of ice, the ice will just melt into slush before it can freeze the cream. To prevent the ice from melting, you need to lower its temperature, too. That's where salt comes in. Salt molecules make it hard for the water molecules to line up, just the way sugar molecules do, so salty ice is colder than unsalty ice. Early ice cream makers layered their ice with salt to keep it cold enough to freeze the ice cream—and it worked. Sweet chemistry!

SCIENCE

We All Scream for Ice Cream

Chocolate, vanilla, and strawberry are just the beginning in ice cream flavors. How about purple yam ice cream? You can eat that in the Philippines. In Iran, you can taste ice cream flavored with rosewater and powdered orchid roots, called salep. The Lebanese make an ice cream with apricot leather. And one old English cookbook even has a recipe for brown-bread ice cream.

DAY 4 THURSDAY

My lunch diary: Track and field tryouts at noon today. Everyone (like me) who isn't trying out is sitting around the playing field or in the bleachers, eating lunch and watching the action. The coach says if there's garbage left behind, the whole school will have to run laps. Fortunately, I've got a minimum-garbage kind of lunch: egg salad in a pita pocket and an apple. Nothing to toss but the apple core. That will go in the school compost bin—if the coach's dog doesn't get it first!

Did the dog get your apple core? He may be a chihuahua but he sure is fast! So you have EGGS, PITA, AND APPLES to look up. Plus, find out about the secret ingredient in your egg salad: MAYONNAISE. That's what makes it egg salad instead of just smashed-up egg.

X-RAY PICTURE OF COACH'S
DOG'S STOMACH AFTER LUNCH

ham sandwich

carrot muffin

apple
(organic)

hot dog

granola bar
(stolen from backpack
when student was
on track)

cookie
(a bit stale)

☐ EGGS
☐ PITA
☐ MAYONNAISE
☐ APPLES

THE YOLK'S on YOU!

How about a crocodile egg for lunch? Or a penguin egg? When we talk about eggs we usually mean chicken eggs, but people have also eaten the eggs of geese, ducks, turkeys, emus, quails, penguins, turtles, and crocodiles. Some eggs are so small they're barely a mouthful, while an ostrich egg could feed a family.

Eggs are a pretty versatile food. They can be poached, scrambled, fried, or made into omelettes, quiches, custards, sauces, and puddings. In 17th-century France and England, something called "poached threads" was a popular dish. People would heat syrup and then drizzle a thin stream of egg yolk into it. The yolk would cook into sweet threads.

The Chinese have a delicacy called "thousand-year-old eggs," or "century eggs," even though it actually takes only months to make them. They're not really that old, they're just preserved. Basically you take duck, chicken, or quail eggs and coat them in a mixture including clay, ash, salt, and lime. You then cover them in soil and leave them in a cool, dark place for about six months. Prepared this way, they'll last about a year. When you crack them open, the egg white looks like jelly and has an amber color, while the yolk is kind of gray-green and gooey. The flavor is strong and earthy—some people say it tastes a bit like cheese.

Oh, hello.

☐ EGGS
☐ PITA
☐ MAYONNAISE
☐ APPLES

PeRfect PackaGiNG

While you were sleeping, we made your breakfast.

Every egg begins as a germ cell. That's not the kind of germ that causes disease. It's a special cell that plays a key part in animal reproduction. In a raw egg, you can still see the germ cell—a tiny white disk, barely as big as the head of a pin, sitting on top of the yolk. A hen's body contains thousands of germ cells that could someday turn into eggs. If the egg is fertilized by a rooster, it will keep growing and turn into a chick. If not, it just remains an egg—and eventually ends up on someone's plate.

As the germ cell matures, it builds a yolk, which is made mainly of fats and proteins. In a fertilized egg, the yolk would hold enough nutrients for the 21 days it takes a chick to develop inside the egg. The color of the yolk depends on what the hen eats. If the egg yolk has a strong yellow color, the hen probably ate corn or alfalfa.

Next, the hen's body creates the white of the egg. You can think of the white as a combination of nutrients and packing material, designed to both nourish and protect the germ cell. The shell comes last, a hard, protective coating made of calcium carbonate and protein. It might look solid, but it's dotted with about 10,000 tiny pores that will let the growing chick breathe. It takes about 14 hours for the hen's body to construct the shell before she finally lays the egg.

All the Same Inside

All eggshells start out white, but they don't all stay that color. While the egg is still inside the chicken, pigments are deposited on the shell. The kind of pigment, and the color of the egg, depends on the breed of the hen. Rhode Island Reds produce brown eggs, Araucana hens produce blue or green eggs, and Speckledy or Maran chickens produce dark-brown speckled eggs. But inside, all chicken eggs look pretty much the same!

LUNCH LAUGHS

Q: What happens when you tell an egg a joke?

A: It CRACKS up.

eDiBLe PLates?

Pita is the ultimate convenience food. You can use it as a plate and spoon as well as food. You can wrap it around meat and vegetables or stuff them inside it. You can use it to scoop up stews or dips, or to mop up sauces or the last of your soup. And you don't have to wash the dishes. You just eat them!

People in the Middle East, northern Africa, and Mediterranean Europe have been using pita for thousands of years. It's a flatbread, probably the first kind of bread invented. You don't need a large oven or a lot of fuel to bake flatbread. A hot stone beside the fire will work, or a cheap, easy-to-build clay oven. The oldest known clay oven—6000 years old—was found in the ruins of the ancient city of Babylon in Iraq, and it still held evidence that it was once used to make flatbread. But flatbread could be far older. Archeologists have turned up evidence of people grinding cattails and ferns into flour as long as 30,000 years ago, in the midst of the last ice age.

Grampa and his buddy have another use for empty pitas

HISTORY

59

PUTTING THE Pocket in the Pita

Bread, you'll never understand, you were just raised differently.

Pita, you're full of hot air.

Pita is what's called a double-layer flatbread, made with yeast. Just like sandwich bread, pita dough is mixed, kneaded, and left to rise. Then it's punched down and most of the bubbles of gas are knocked out of it. At this point, sandwich bread would be placed in a loaf pan and allowed to rise again. Then it would be baked slowly at medium heat to keep the small bubble spaces intact.

Pita, on the other hand, is patted flat and round like a pancake, and then popped into a very hot oven to bake quickly. The moisture inside the dough turns into steam, runs together into one big bubble, and puffs the bread up. Because the oven is so hot, the bread finishes baking before the steam bubble collapses, so the bread has a pocket that's just right for stuffing with other foods.

☑ EGGS
☑ PITA
☐ MAYONNAISE
☐ APPLES

A CULINARY TRIUMPH!

The year was 1756, and the French army, commanded by the Duc de Richelieu, had just captured the city of Mahón on the Mediterranean island of Minorca. The duke's chef was preparing a victory feast, which included a rich sauce made of cream and eggs. Disaster! The kitchen was out of cream. In desperation, the chef substituted olive oil and hoped for the best. His creation was a hit. He named the new sauce Mahonnaise, to honor the duke's military triumph, but an early cookbook writer spelled it wrong and it's been "mayonnaise" ever since.

Mayonnaise went from being a fancy sauce to an everyday ingredient a century ago. About 1910, New York delicatessen owner Richard Hellman started selling his wife Nina's version of mayonnaise to his customers. The sauce was a hit, and within a couple of years Richard had built a big plant to produce Hellman's mayonnaise and was distributing it with his own fleet of trucks. Bottled mayonnaise soon showed up in households nationwide. It's still a common addition to sandwiches and salads throughout North America and Europe.

I hope the duke doesn't notice...

This will be the greatest victory feast ever!

OIL

VIN

GLOBS AND DROPLets

Mayonnaise is a mixture called an emulsion.

That's what you get when you put together two liquids that don't dissolve into each other. To see what an emulsion looks like, put some water (half a cup is plenty) in a clear jar or bottle with a tight-fitting lid. Then drop in about a tablespoon of cooking oil. See how the oil globs together? If you leave it to sit, more and more globs appear and merge until all the oil is floating on top of the water. If, however, you make sure the lid is on tight and then shake the container hard, the oil breaks into small drops and spreads through the water. That's an emulsion.

The tricky thing with emulsions is to keep them from globbing back into two separate liquids again. If you leave your shaken oil and water for a while, that's exactly what will happen. In mayonnaise, olive oil and vinegar are the two liquids in the emulsion, and they don't mix any better than oil and water. The magic ingredient—the thing that keeps them from separating—is egg yolk. It's called an emulsifier, and it coats the droplets of oil and vinegar with a thin layer that stops them from globbing into larger droplets. It works best if the droplets are tiny, so making mayonnaise involves a lot of whipping and whisking to keep the droplets small.

See? I told you it would be fun to get out and mingle.

A Sweeter Fruit

The ancestors of all the world's apples grew in the mountains of Kazakhstan, on the borderline between Europe and Asia. Kazakhstan's former capital city is named Almaty, which means "the Father of Apples." Those early apples were probably small and sour, like modern crab apples, but gradually people bred larger, sweeter ones, and began trading them with their neighbors. And they spread throughout the world. The apple in your lunch might come from Europe, North America, Australia, New Zealand, South Africa, or almost anywhere.

Over the centuries, plant breeders and apple lovers have bred a huge variety of apples for different purposes. Some of them have names that make you want to take a big bite—like Honey Crisp and Coconut Crunch. Others, not so much—care for a Leathercoat, or an Arkansas Black? Apples come in plenty of colors, too. On the outside, they can be red, yellow, white, pink, green, or almost black, and inside they vary just as much.

HISTORY

THURSDAY

Q: What did the mayonnaise say to the refrigerator?

a: Close the door, I'm dressing!

Apple Magic

Apples turn up in a lot of stories, and they often mean trouble. According to the Greek poet Homer, the Trojan War began when a goddess gave the Apple of Discord to Paris, prince of Troy. In Norse mythology, the goddess Idun guards a casket of golden apples that can restore power to the gods if their strength starts to fade. And in the Grimm Brothers' fairy tale, Snow White is fed a poisoned apple by her wicked stepmother.

aGeD TO PeRfection

Freshly picked fruit usually tastes best, but that's not always true of apples. As long as they are stored properly—in a cool place—apples can be edible, and sometimes even tastier, months later. That's part of what made the apple a popular fruit in the days before trucks and trains rushed fruit to market, and refrigerators kept it fresh.

The secret is malic acid, the chemical compound that gives many unripe fruits a sour taste. As the fruits ripen, chemical changes reduce the amount of malic acid and the fruits become less sour. In many varieties of apples, that chemical process continues even after the apple is picked. An apple that has been sitting in storage for a few weeks might actually be sweeter than it was when it left the tree.

We just keep getting sweeter, but you grapefruits will always be sour.

SCIENCE

DAY 5 FRiDay

My lunch diary: End of the school week, and I'm more than halfway through this assignment. Today's lunch is special. Last month we had a reading challenge at school. The class that read the most books in two weeks would get a pizza lunch, paid for— and delivered in person—by the principal. My class won, and today's the day. She promised lots of different kinds. Fingers crossed for no anchovies or olives, though!

Congratulations on the big win! Now, find me some information on PIZZA. We'll divide up the toppings, too. You can research PEPPERS AND ONIONS. AND HERBS. Did you know there were herbs in pizza?

66

☐ **PIZZA**
☐ **PEPPERS**
☐ **ONIONS**
☐ **HERBS**

FROM ITALY,
WiTH TOPPiNGS

candy sprinkles

pine nuts

chorizo sausage

fresh pineapple

cookie bits

spicy meatballs

melted aged Gouda

thin crust

Even though it comes from Italy, pizza owes its worldwide popularity to American soldiers. During World War II, the American soldiers stationed in southern Italy discovered a local street food called pizza: flatbread topped with oil, tomato sauce, herbs, garlic, and—sometimes—cheese.

The soldiers loved it. And when they came home after the war, they were surprised to discover that pizza had been available in the United States for years, mainly from small shops in Italian neighborhoods. The Italian immigrants who owned those shops suddenly found they had a brand-new, much larger group of customers. That was the beginning of the pizza boom that has since spread around the world.

As pizza grew in popularity. people began to add more and more ingredients. Some were traditional Italian foods, such as pepperoni, mushrooms, onions, and anchovies. Some were new and a lot more unusual, like pineapple, satay chicken, or refried beans. Soon you could have a whole meal perched on a pizza!

UNDERCOVER INGREDIENTS

There's really nothing wrong with most pizza ingredients. Bread's okay, and so is tomato sauce. Onions, peppers, mushrooms, tomatoes, ham, sausage, cheese—those are all good things. But some things that aren't so good for you can sneak into pizza in disguise. Commercial pizzas usually contain a lot more fat and salt than you realize—and too much fat (or oil) and salt isn't good for your body. Pizza crust has oil in it. Cheese has fat—a lot of fat. So do sausages like pepperoni or salami. Tomato sauce often contains oil, too.

There's also salt in most of those ingredients, especially the cheese, sausage, and sauce. If a slice of pizza makes you thirsty, it's a good bet that it contains plenty of salt.

So, if eating too much commercial pizza is unhealthy (and expensive), how about making your own? All you need is some kind of flatbread and your choice of toppings. You can even invent a brand-new recipe. Peanut butter and raisin pizza, anyone?

— garlic pickles

— organic vine-ripened tomato

bubblegum ice cream

— meat patty

My brand-new pizza recipe

SCIENCE

69

Sign on a pizza shop window

SEVEN DAYS
WITHOUT
PIZZA MAKES
ONE WEAK

MARIO'S PIZZA

... Even my fingers are exhausted.

The Traveling Pizza

Pizza is popular around the world because it's so easy to adapt to local tastes. All you have to do is change the toppings. Hawaiians add pineapple and banana. The Japanese add boiled eggs, bits of fish, and, occasionally, squid ink. Kuwaitis like grilled, spiced meat and hummus (chickpea dip) on their pizza. In Brazil, you can order pizza with quail eggs and chocolate.

banana peppers

Scotch bonnet
chili peppers

Thai
peppers

cayenne chili
peppers

bell peppers

The Prada
jalapeño
pepper hat

THE Name GAME

The colorful peppers you slice and put on your pizza aren't even distantly related to the black pepper from India you put in your grinder. But when Columbus stumbled upon America, it was black pepper he was looking for, so when he found Native Americans using a hot spice, he called it pepper, too. And the name stuck.

Chili peppers—as American peppers, hot or mild, are more accurately called—spread so far and so fast that Europeans lost track of where they came from. Hot chili peppers became so important in Indian food that Europeans started to believe they originated in Asia, just like black pepper. Now we know better. Archeological and genetic studies show that the first chili peppers came from South America, somewhere south of the Amazon.

HISTORY

FOOD on FiRe!

Not all chili peppers are hot. Bell peppers, such as the green peppers on top of pizza, have a mild, fresh flavor with no real bite. But there's another kind of pepper lurking in your slice. The spicy bite in pizza sauce often comes from dried red chili peppers, which have a more fiery taste. Sometimes you will see shakers of dried pepper flakes at a pizza stand. That's because lots of people like to add the right amount of heat to suit their taste.

The fire in peppers comes from capsaicin, a chemical that protects the chili pepper's seeds. It's only released when the seeds are chewed or ground up, but then things can get really hot. The United States uses a system called Scoville heat units to give an approximate measure of spiciness. Bell peppers, with very little capsaicin, score 0 units. Spicy jalapeños clock in between 2500 and 5000 units, and super-hot habanero peppers can hit 300,000 units.

And what if you get too much capsaicin? An ice cube or cool liquid, especially milk, can ease the immediate burn on your lips and tongue. Something rough, such as rice or crackers, will help by distracting the nerves that are sending the too-hot signals. Or just wipe your streaming eyes and wait. The capsaicin burn will fade in about 15 minutes.

Habanero pepper, 300,000 Scoville units.

YIKES. I need a fire extinguisher...

MAGIC on the MenU

Onions probably originated somewhere in the northern hemisphere, but they've been on the worldwide menu for so long that no one really knows for sure. Today they're found in everything from Vietnamese noodle soup to Indian curry to North American hamburgers. And, of course, they make a delicious topping for pizza.

In some times and places, onions were more than food. The ancient Egyptians saw the onion as a symbol of eternal life and believed that the smell of an onion could bring back the dead. And garlic is a relative of the onion—one with links to evil magic. Long ago, Greek travelers left piles of garlic at crossroads to confuse any demons that might be following them. And everyone knows garlic keeps vampires away, right?

HISTORY

73

FRIDAY

BEFORE

AFTER:
NO MORE TEARS

Put on your swim goggles.

A LITTLE AFTER THE AFTER

Don't stop there! You can put on your swim cap, bathing suit, and flippers, too!

DRiVen TO Tears

If you start chopping up onions, soon everyone in the kitchen will be weeping. The stuff that makes your eyes run is sulfur, and onions use it as a chemical weapon.

As an onion grows, it collects sulfur from the soil and stores it inside its cells. Each cell also contains another chemical, an enzyme, inside a tiny package. When you slice an onion, the cells are damaged. The package containing the enzyme breaks open, and the enzyme attacks the chemical compounds that hold the sulfur. Strong sulfur-laden molecules escape into the air—and into your eyes and nose.

The compound that makes your eyes run is called a lachrymator (the word for something that triggers tears). It irritates the nerves in the eyes and nose. The result is a runny nose, pouring eyes, and a strong desire to get the onion into the frying pan as quickly as possible.

A Cure Worse than the Disease

Pliny the Elder was a Roman writer and naturalist who lived almost 2000 years ago. He wrote that onions are good for your eyes because the tears caused by the smell of the onion will cure poor vision. Even more effective, he said, was to squeeze the juice from an onion and apply it directly to the eyes. Ouch!

OREGANO AIRLINES

WHAT IS THAT WONDERFUL SMELL?

You can smell pizza long before you see it, that delicious cheesy, spicy, eat-me-now aroma. Some of the smell comes from the crust and the toppings, but a lot of it comes from herbs—those little dark-green flecks in the sauce.

The most common herb in pizza sauce is oregano. It comes from a Mediterranean plant that has traveled around the world with pizza and other Italian creations like lasagna. Before Italian-style foods were so popular, oregano was mostly used—at least outside of Italy —as a medicine. Medieval apothecaries prescribed oregano tea to aid digestion and reduce gas—which could be handy if you eat too much pizza!

Other herbs you might find in your pizza sauce include basil, thyme, and sage. They're all bits of dried plant with one thing in common: a powerful aroma.

HISTORY

Here comes the oregano! Hold up your pizzas.

Basil

thyme

76

A Nose-full of Taste

We taste foods through the taste buds on our tongues, but all our tongues really tell us is whether a food is sweet, sour, salty, bitter, or savory. To tell the difference between similar things—beef and lamb, or carrots and turnips—we also use the odor receptors in our noses.

If you've ever had a cold that plugged your nose completely, you know how dull your food tasted, and it wasn't just because you were sick. Even an apple and an onion taste alike if you can't smell them. If you're brave enough, you can test this. Plug your nose, close your eyes, and get someone to give you a small piece of apple to eat and a small piece of onion. Can you tell which is which? Bet you can't!

The herbs in pizza work on your nose just as the pizza fills your mouth. Your brain adds the two kinds of information together and comes up with the pizza flavor you're used to.

Don't peek!

sage

DAY 6 saturday

My lunch diary: This is what my mom calls "one of those days"—too many things going on at once. She took me to my swimming lesson this morning, and the soccer tournament starts in half an hour. No time to go home, so we're eating lunch on a bench at the soccer field. Mom made peanut butter and banana spirals—one of my favorites. You spread peanut butter on a tortilla, wrap it around a banana, and slice it into sushi-shaped pieces. Plus, my dad baked last night, so we have spice cookies. To keep our energy levels up, he said.

Your spirals sound like fun, but not for me. I'm allergic to peanuts. How about finding out more about PEANUTS, BANANAS, AND TORTILLAS? And pick a couple of the SPICES in spice cookies — where they come from, how they work, that kind of thing.

LUNCH LAUGHS

Q: Why did the fisherman put peanut butter on a hook?

a: He wanted to catch a jellyfish!

Open wider!

WHen iS a NUt NOT A Nut?

When it's a vegetable, of course!

Peanuts are confusing. They're called nuts, but they're actually legumes, which means they're in the same vegetable family as peas and beans. And another odd thing about peanuts? They grow upside down. Peanut plants have flowers that appear above ground, like most flowers. But then the stems bend down and push the fruits—the peanuts—under the ground to grow and mature.

Hiding its fruit underground is an advantage for the peanut. In some parts of the world, locusts and other insects can descend on fields in such numbers that entire crops are destroyed. But the peanut, with its fruit safely tucked away out of reach, survives. So do the people who rely on it for food.

You'd have to be nuts to live up there.

Peanuts started out in South America, in Brazil. The Portuguese took them to Africa, India, and Asia in the 16th century. Then they came back across the ocean—this time to North America—aboard slave ships from Africa. In the southern United States people still call peanuts "goober peas," which comes from *nguba*, an African word for peanut.

HISTORY 80

Peanut PROBLEMS

Peanuts are full of protein, which makes them especially important in countries where protein is hard to come by and malnutrition is a danger. The soybean is the only plant that has more protein, but peanuts are cheaper to produce.

SMOOTH AND YUMMY PEANUT BUTTER

WARNING

DO NOT CONSUME IF YOU HAVE A PEANUT ALLERGY. MAY CAUSE HIVES, ITCHING, SNEEZING, OR DEATH.

However, peanuts also belong to a small group of foods—many of them nuts—that can trigger severe allergic reactions. The reaction is probably caused by proteins, but which ones? Peanuts hold more than 30 different proteins, so it's difficult to pinpoint the ones that cause the problem.

The effects of a peanut allergy can range from extremely unpleasant to fatal. At the unpleasant end, they include hives, a runny nose and sneezing, itchiness, and swelling. The most severe reaction is anaphylaxis (*ah-nah-fil-AX-is*). Swelling in the throat can block breathing and the body can go into shock. Without treatment, the allergy sufferer can die. For some people, just smelling a peanut will trigger that kind of extreme reaction.

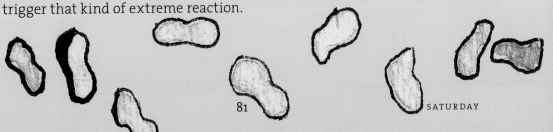

THE COMPANY FRUIT

Bananas are great travelers. People were growing them in Papua New Guinea 5000 years ago, and they've been moving on ever since, to Egypt, India, all around the Pacific Ocean, and even to Europe.

They became a worldwide hit when a huge American corporation, the United Fruit Company, began growing them for export in 1899.

The United Fruit Company owned plantations all over Central America, as well as rail lines and a large fleet of steamships that carried the bananas to market. It was so wealthy and powerful that it controlled the governments of many of the banana-growing countries for decades and ran the countries for the benefit of the banana trade. That's where the term "banana republic" comes from.

About 35 years ago, a combination of natural disasters and political change put the United Fruit Company out of business, although many of its banana plantations still exist and still provide bananas to the world.

HISTORY

SCIENCE

WRAPPED TO GO

Move over, buddy, you're making me ripe.

PEACHES $1.29/lb

BANANAS .99/lb

Bananas come naturally pre-packaged and bundled for shipping. They grow in clusters on stout stems, and they're protected by thick skins. An entire stem of bananas can be picked at once and packed in a shipping container. Bananas are picked green and gradually ripen on the journey to your door. By the time they're ripe, the tough skins have turned into much softer wrappings that peel off easily.

As a banana ripens, its starch is converted into sugar—in a big way. Green bananas have 25 times as much starch as sugar, but ripe bananas have more than 20 times as much sugar as starch. Like most fruits, bananas give off ethylene gas as they ripen—it's part of the recognizable smell of ripe fruit. Bananas give off more ethylene gas than any other fruit, so much that the gas can actually trigger ripening in the fruit around them. One handy trick to getting green fruit to ripen is to put it in a paper bag along with a banana.

LUNCH LAUGHS

Q: What do you get if you throw two banana peels on the floor?

a: A pair of slippers.

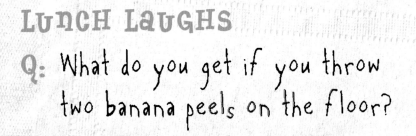

☑ PEANUTS
☑ BANANAS
☐ TORTILLAS
☐ SPICES

BORN IN America

Tortillas are yet another kind of bread, one invented in the corn-growing regions of the Americas, long ago. When the Spanish arrived and saw the local breads, they named them tortillas, which means small, round cakes.

A tortilla is a true flatbread, with no yeast or leavening agent added. It doesn't rise like sandwich bread or puff up like pita. It just lies there, round and flat and useful, ready to become a plate, a wrapper, a scoop, or a handy snack, all on its own.

Originally, all tortillas were made from ground corn, the basic grain of the Americas. Corn tortillas are still an important food, especially in Mexico and parts of the southwestern United States, but other kinds of tortillas have joined them. Europeans brought wheat and wheat flour to North America, and flour tortillas were invented. Today tortillas are made from both corn and wheat flour, and with added ingredients such as spinach, tomato, or jalapeños. And they're used to wrap foods their Native American inventors never dreamed of. Such as bananas!

SATURDAY

What your tortilla is doing when you think it's just lying there

meditating ommmmm	doing math 25 x 6 - 37.6 + 2385	planning supper	thinking about Christmas

Things your tortilla does when you are not looking

downward-facing dog

stomach curls to tighten core muscles

tree pose

smiling at other tortillas

(this is VERY HARD for a tortilla so never disturb it in this pose)

TRiCKS of tHe TRaDe

You can't just take a bunch of dried corn kernels,

grind them up, and turn them into tortillas. Native American cooks figured that out millennia ago. The problem is the tough hulls on corn kernels. Think of grinding up unpopped popcorn, and you get the idea. It would be hard, slow work. The other problem is that straight ground corn doesn't stick together in a dough.

Long ago, Native Americans discovered the answer to both problems. You can get the corn hulls to soften and peel away by cooking the kernels in an alkaline solution made by mixing water and a little ash from the fire (commonly called lime water). The remaining kernels can then be ground into a dough-like material called masa. As an added benefit, the corn is now even more nutritious. The lime water reacts with the corn, making some of its vitamins easier to digest, and lime water itself adds valuable calcium to the masa.

In the old days, the cook would grind the masa and knead it until it was soft and stretchy. Then she would pat it flat and cook the tortilla quickly on a very hot surface. Today, masa is produced in factories, flash-dried, and sold as masa harina, a sort of quick tortilla mix. Just add water and fry.

87

FLAVORS TO DIE FOR?

People died because of spices.

The ones who suffered the most were the people who lived on the Spice Islands of Southeast Asia. The Spice Islands were once the only source of nutmeg and cloves, two spices that fetched huge prices in Europe. Today, the islands are part of Indonesia, but a few centuries ago they belonged to anyone strong enough to take them. Many did.

The islanders traded both nutmeg and cloves with China and other Asian nations, but as demand for the spices grew, outsiders tried to take over. First, it was the Arabs. Then the Portuguese, English, and Dutch squabbled over the islands and the spice trade. In the 1600s, the Dutch won. They destroyed nutmeg and clove trees on any islands they didn't control, and executed anyone who defied them. They hung on to control of the trade until 1770, when a French botanist finally smuggled both nutmeg and clove plants out of Dutch territory and started growing them on a French-owned island.

By then, most of the Spice Islanders had been killed, enslaved, or exiled. The death toll was in the thousands.

TOO MUCH
OF A GOOD THING?

nutmeg stretching

Nutmeg is the seed of one tree native to the Spice Islands, and cloves are the dried, unopened flower buds from another tree. They're often used in sweet things, such as spice cookies and puddings, but also in curries, roasts, and stews. As with herbs, we taste them more with our noses than with our tongues.

Nutmeg has been used as medicine as well as spice. In Indian tradition, a tiny amount of nutmeg was rubbed on a baby's lips to help it sleep. Modern Indian researchers are investigating whether nutmeg might be a source of medicines to fight cancer and liver disease. But nutmeg has a dark side, too. Too much nutmeg— far more than you would ever use in a batch of cookies —can make you sick. And *way* too much nutmeg can even kill you.

cloves out for a walk after supper

nutmeg contemplating his homework

nutmeg on holiday

SCIENCE

cloves up nose
— mmm, fresh!

Cloves have a particularly strong and pleasant smell, which is one of the reasons they have always been so popular. In the days when sewage and garbage were dumped in the streets, wealthy people liked to block out the smell with bundles of perfumes and spices held under their noses, and cloves worked beautifully. People still use cloves to help with toothaches, because they contain an ingredient called eugenol that both numbs the pain and acts as an antiseptic. It's no substitute for a visit to the dentist, though!

stinky garbage and sewage

Tasty Medicine

An American researcher who was testing various foods on people with diabetes was surprised to discover that apple pie reduced their blood sugar levels, even though the pie contained plenty of sugar. Eventually, he realized the effect came from the cinnamon in the pie. Just a quarter of a teaspoon of cinnamon a day, he found, reduced his patients' blood sugar levels substantially.

DAY 7 SUNDAY

My lunch diary: Last day of the assignment, and this is going to be a great lunch. We're going to the zoo, and then we're having a picnic with my cousins. Our parents are packing a feast. I see cold chicken, potato salad, and corn on the cob. Corn's so much better outside, where the butter can just drip on the grass. And chocolate brownies for dessert. Great way to finish the weekend!

Hope it was a good day and a great picnic. For your last bit of research, find out something about CHICKEN, POTATOES, AND CORN. Your potato salad would have mayonnaise in it, too, but we've already looked at that, so add CHOCOLATE to your list of topics. Chocolate's always a good way to top off a meal—or an assignment!

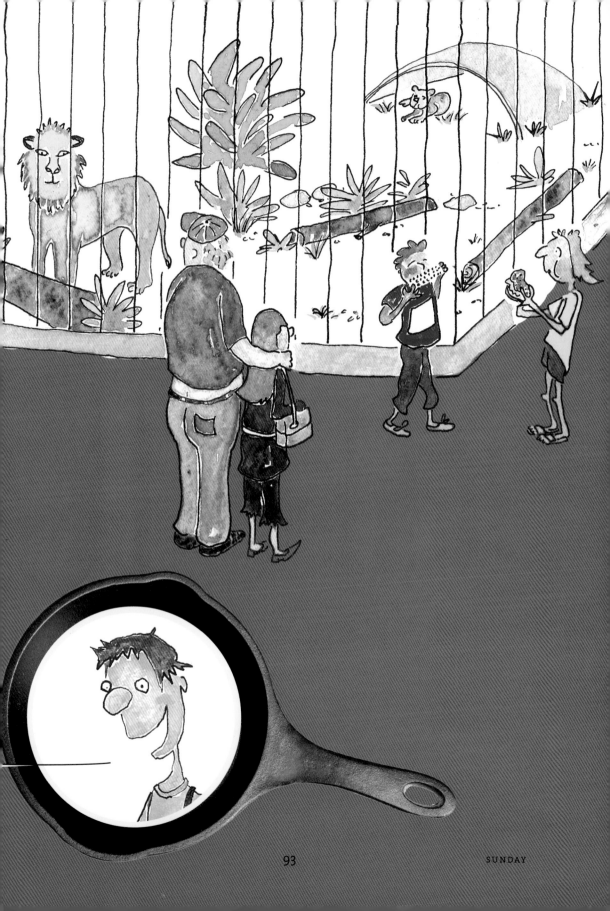

93 SUNDAY

FOWL WITH FLAIR

People have been eating chicken for thousands of years, and in almost every corner of the world. Over all that time, they've developed some creative recipes, and creative names, for a chicken lunch.

In northern England in the Middle Ages, people made a colorful dish called Hindle wakes when they wanted something special for a festival. That was chicken stuffed with spiced prunes, served cold and decorated with parsley and other greens.

In the Solomon Islands, they make tampumpie. The chicken is cooked in a stone oven, surrounded by sliced taro or yams, and covered with lots of grated coconut.

Coronation chicken was invented for the coronation of Queen Elizabeth II in 1953. It's slices of cold chicken served with curried mayonnaise and apricots.

Chicken coronation

Coronation Chicken

A fairly recent dish in North America and Europe is the turducken. That's a chicken stuffed inside a duck stuffed inside a turkey and roasted. Turducken is a modest version of a dish that's been around since Roman times. In those days, for great banquets, chefs would stuff a dozen or more birds, one inside the other, from a swan right down to a tiny sparrow.

HISTORY

SUNDAY

THE BiGGeR, THE BetteR!

In the old days, the chicken on your table was a lot smaller than it is today. Then, in the 19th century, a different, bigger breed of chicken arrived in Europe and America from China. People liked what they saw—and ate!

Chicken in the old days

Customers wanted big chickens, with plenty of white meat, and breeders were happy to oblige. They crossed chicken varieties in search of the ideal chicken and discarded varieties that didn't meet the standard. Gradually, there were fewer and fewer different kinds of chickens on farms. Today, the most common kind of chicken is a large, fast-growing bird developed from a cross between an English breed and an American breed.

There's a danger in putting all your eggs in one chicken basket. If a disease attacks the dominant breed (and that sort of thing has happened before), we could lose most of the chickens we depend on for meat and eggs. For that reason, breeders and scientists are trying to preserve older breeds of chickens, with different immunities to disease, as insurance for the future.

Chicken today

HISTORY

BURieD TReaSURe

When the Spanish adventurer Francisco Pizarro conquered the empire of the Incas in 1532, he was after its gold. He had no idea that he'd discovered something even more valuable—the potato. Almost five centuries later, potatoes are big business. People eat potatoes just about everywhere and in every possible way. In 2006, India and China alone produced almost 100 million metric tons of potatoes. That's enough to fill a train stretching from Toronto, Canada, to Melbourne, Australia.

But the potato was not an instant success in Europe. Because potatoes were cheap and easy to grow, some governments saw them only as suitable food for prisoners and people in workhouses, who had no choice. Oddly, that was the key to their success in France.

A French army officer who had been a prisoner of war in Germany developed a taste for potatoes while in prison there. When he returned to France, he managed to convince King Louis XVI of their value. He was so successful that the queen, Marie Antoinette, even wore potato flowers as a decoration on her dress. That made the potato fashionable, and it was on its way.

something FOR everyone

Most of the potatoes used around the world are descended from just a few of the varieties created by Incan farmers. The Incas took a small, bumpy root and developed scores of variations, suitable for different growing conditions, tastes, and nutritional needs.

Let's buzz off, guys. We don't want to stick around here.

Peruvian Indians, descendants of those Incan farmers, have about 200 words for the different kinds of potatoes found in the Andes. There are potato varieties that have different flavors and colors, are more nutritious, survive cold weather better, or have other special properties. Some Andean potatoes are natural insect traps. Their leaves are covered with fragile hairs that break when even the smallest insect lands on them. The broken hairs release a sticky goo that glues the insect to the leaf. And there it stays until it dies, trapped just a few steps away from a delicious meal.

SCIENCE

99

SUNDAY

A Blessing and a Curse

When potatoes reached Ireland, they became the chief food of the Irish poor. A small plot of land, planted with potatoes, could feed a family. The menu was boring, but fairly nutritious: boiled potatoes, washed down with sips of buttermilk. Then, in 1845, a disease called blight hit the Irish potato crop, causing the potatoes to rot in the fields. Within a decade, about 4 out of every 10 people had died of starvation or related illnesses, or had left Ireland forever.

WHAT'S IN A name?

In most of the world, the vegetable North Americans call corn is known as maize. The name corn comes from the earliest English settlers. In British English, corn just means grain. When English-language speakers arrived in America, they saw Native Americans as far north as Canada using maize in the same way Europeans used grains like wheat and barley. So, the English settlers called it corn.

Corn was so important to Native Americans that it became part of their stories about the creation of the world and of humankind. According to the Maya of southern Mexico, the gods shaped the first men out of white and yellow corn. The Incas told the story of the son and daughter of the sun god, who led the people to a fertile land and taught them how to grow corn.

Corn has become just as important in places far away from its origins. In Kenya in southern Africa, for example, everybody—rich or poor—eats cornmeal and corn flour. One of the most popular basic foods is *ugali*, which is cornmeal boiled into a thick, sticky porridge. Today, corn is the world's third-largest food crop, after wheat and rice.

Don't get too close or you may pop!

☑ CHICKEN
☑ POTATOES
☑ **CORN**
☐ CHOCOLATE

SCIENCE

YOU WANT IT?
PLANT IT!

OTHER USES FOR DELICIOUS CORN:

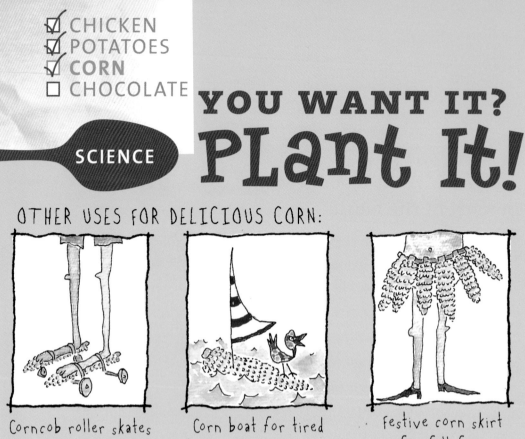

Corncob roller skates

Corn boat for tired birds crossing oceans

Festive corn skirt for fall fairs

It doesn't look like it, but corn is actually a kind of grass. More than 8000 years ago, somewhere in what is now Mexico, people began making changes to a grass called teosinte. They picked the best plants, the ones with lots of large kernels, and planted their seeds. When they harvested the new crop, they saved the seeds from the plants they liked best and used them to plant the next year's crop. Over many generations, they turned teosinte into maize, or corn.

Modern corn is very different from teosinte. Its huge seed head, packed with juicy kernels, comes wrapped thickly in tough husks. It's easy for humans to pick, store, and shuck, and it produces more food per plant than any other grain. But at a price. Because the kernels are packed so tightly together, corn can no longer seed itself. Without people to plant it, corn would disappear.

THE EMPEROR'S FAVORITE DRINK

Like so many of our foods, chocolate originally came from Central and South America. Its source is the cacao tree, which grew in hot, humid river valleys near the equator. Sometime in the distant past, people carried the tree's large seed pods northwards. And that's when chocolate really took off.

HISTORY

The farmers of the Olmec civilization were growing cacao trees in what is now Mexico about 3000 years ago. They introduced cacao beans to the Maya, and the Maya sold cacao to the Aztecs. By the time Spanish invaders reached the Aztec court of Moctezuma II in 1519, chocolate drinks made from cacao beans were an important part of religious rituals and a favorite with the emperor and his court. One Spaniard reported that servants brought 50 jars of foaming chocolate at a time to the emperor and his guests, and that Moctezuma drank his chocolate from a golden cup.

When the Spanish conquered the Aztecs they took over the cacao plantations and turned them into big moneymakers. In the 16th and 17th centuries, with chocolate hugely popular in Europe, cacao was Spain's most important export crop.

LUNCH LAUGHS

Q: Why don't they serve chocolate in prison?

a: Because it makes you break out!

MAKING IT Sweet!

If you bit into a fresh-picked cacao bean, you'd be disappointed. The beans have to be processed before they get that rich chocolate flavor. Harvesters cut pods from the trees, split them open, and remove the damp beans, which are piled together in big wooden boxes. There they sit for up to seven days, while microbes produced in a process called fermentation change some of the carbohydrates in the beans to alcohol. The alcohol kills the beans so that they can't sprout, and the fermentation process changes their color to chocolate brown. Then the beans are spread in the sun to dry. The alcohol is long gone by the time the beans dry out.

The dry cacao beans are roasted, crushed, and ground into a sticky paste—the basic ingredient of cocoa powder, chocolate bars, and all the other chocolate delights people have invented. Among the ingredients people add to chocolate are sugar, honey, vanilla, chili peppers, milk, and almonds. And not all chocolate creations are sweet. In Mexico, spicy mole (*moh-lay*) sauce is made with unsweetened chocolate, and sometimes chocolate is added to European stews to give the gravy a richer flavor.

Best combination: chocolate and ME!

SCIENCE

SUNDAY

DesseRt!
OuR Top 10 FooD Facts

The lunch assignment turned out to be fun—and one of the best parts was all the fascinating, funny, and just plain weird information we dug up. Lots of what we found was too good to throw away, so the class decided to make a top 10 list to share with the entire school. And here it is!

OUR TOP 10 **FAVORITE,** Fantastic, and Fun Food Facts
Starting with Number 10. . . drumroll!

10. Popcorn Fact: Archeologists have found popcorn kernels in 3000-year-old campfire ashes. Aztecs, Incas, and some indigenous North Americans all ate popcorn, and 19th-century Americans even ate it as breakfast cereal.

9. Honey Fact: The ancient Egyptians used honey to treat wounds, just as we might use antibiotic ointment today. And it really works! The honey blocks out air and prevents germs from reaching the wound.

8. Bread Fact: In medieval Europe, you could have your bread and eat it, too. Dry bread was cut into rectangles called trenchers to use as plates. At the end of the meal, you could eat the bread with all the sauces soaked into it, feed it to the animals, or give it away to the poor.

7. Carrot Fact: The bagged baby carrots you buy in grocery stores, washed and ready for snacking, are rarely babies. Usually they're full-sized carrots that have been peeled and whittled down to a "baby" shape and size.

I'm not half the carrot I used to be.

Hey, dude, how much you want for that can of caviar?

500 cheeseburgers with extra mayo.

6. Egg Fact: The most expensive eggs in the world are salted fish eggs called caviar, and they come from the sturgeon, a fish that can grow as long as two bathtubs placed end to end. A soup can filled with caviar would cost about the same as 500 hamburgers.

5. Grain Fact: Ergot is a poisonous fungus that grows on grain. Bread contaminated with ergot can cause hallucinations, convulsions, a painful burning in your arms and legs, and worse. In the Middle Ages, the symptoms of ergot poisoning were often blamed on witches or black magic.

4. Insect Fact: A common Aboriginal bush food in parts of Australia is witchetty grubs, picked fresh off a witchetty bush. The grubs are moth larvae, each about the size of a man's thumb. They're said to taste buttery when raw, and a bit like scrambled eggs when they're cooked.

3. Chili Pepper Fact: In India, villagers use chili peppers to keep elephants out of their crops and homes. They make chili balls from crushed hot chilis mixed with elephant dung and burn them when the elephants get too near. The chili-pepper smoke is just too much for those great big elephant noses, and the elephants head back to the forest.

2. Vegetable Fact: The Vegetable Orchestra is a group of Austrian musicians who play instruments made from fresh vegetables. They've made a violin out of a leek, a guitar from celery, a horn from a green pepper, flutes from hollowed-out carrots, and a pumpkin drum played with carrot drumsticks.

And finally...

1. GROSS FACT: Some foods take a yucky route to the table. Honey is bee vomit, bird's nest soup is made from bird spit, and the world's rarest and most expensive coffee is made from coffee beans eaten and pooped out by a catlike animal called a palm civet.

Bon Appetit!

Further Reading

Edible: An Illustrated Guide to the World's Food Plants. Washington, DC: National Geographic Books, 2008.

Pollan, Michael. *The Omnivore's Dilemma for Kids: The Secrets Behind What You Eat*. New York: Dial Press, 2009.

Thornhill, Jan. *Who Wants Pizza? A Kids' Guide to the History, Science and Culture of Food*. Toronto: Maple Tree Press, 2010.

Wishinsky, Frieda, and Elizabeth MacLeod. *Everything but the Kitchen Sink: Weird Stuff You Didn't Know about Food*. Markham, ON: Scholastic, 2008.

Zinczenko, David. *Eat This, Not That! For Kids!* Emmaus, PA: Rodale Books, 2008.

Selected Bibliography

Bernstein, William J. *A Splendid Exchange: How Trade Shaped the World*. New York: Grove Press, 2008.

de Villiers, Marq, and Sheila Hirtle. *Timbuktu: The Sahara's Fabled City of Gold*. New York: Walker, 2007.

Fankhauser, David B. "Rennet for Making Cheese" (last modified November 23, 2009). Available from: biology.clc.uc.edu/fankhauser/cheese/rennet/rennet.html. Accessed August 29, 2010.

Farrell, Kenneth T. *Spices, Condiments, and Seasonings*, 2nd edition. New York: Van Nostrand Reinhold, 1990.

Fernández-Armesto, Felipe. *Food: A History*. London: MacMillan, 2001.

Fraser, Evan D.G., and Andrew Rimas. *Empires of Food: Feast, Famine, and the Rise and Fall of Civilizations*. New York: The Free Press, 2010.

Gies, Frances and Joseph. *Life in a Medieval Village*. New York: Harper & Row, 1990.

Gollner, Adam Leith. *The Fruit Hunters*. Toronto: Doubleday Canada, 2008.

Haber, Barbara. *From Hardtack to Home Fries: An Uncommon History of American Cooks and Meals*. New York: The Free Press, 2002.

Hiddins, Les. *Bush Tucker Field Guide*. Ringwood, Australia: ABC Books, 2001.

Krondl, Michael. *The Taste of Conquest: The Rise and Fall of the Three Great Cities of Spice*. New York: Ballantine Books, 2007.

Kurlansky, Mark, ed. *Choice Cuts: A Savory Selection of Food Writing from Around the World and Throughout History*. New York: Penguin Books, 2002.

Kurlansky, Mark. *Salt: A World History*. Toronto: Vintage Canada, 2002.

Lane, John. *A Taste of the Past*. Newton Abbot, UK: David & Charles, 2004.

Majumdar, Simon. *Eat My Globe: One Year to Go Everywhere and Eat Everything*. New York: The Free Press, 2009.

McGee, Harold. *On Food and Cooking: The Science and Lore of the Kitchen*, 1st revised edition. New York: Scribner, 2004.

Mortimer, Ian. *The Time Traveller's Guide to Medieval England*. London: Vintage, 2009.

National Geographic. *Edible: An Illustrated Guide to the World's Food Plants*. Washington, DC: National Geographic, 2008.

Nieuwoudt, Stephanie. "Growing Maize Is Not What It Used to Be," IPS News Agency, May 27, 2007. Available from: ipsnews.net/news.asp?idnews=37771. Accessed August 31, 2010.

Old Log Church Museum. "The Bishop Who Ate His Boots: The Full Story," 2002. Available from: www.virtualmuseum.ca/Exhibitions/BishopStringer/english/fullstory.html. Accessed August 30, 2010.

Reunionweb. "La fécondation de la vanille par Edmond Albius." Available from: reunionweb.org/decouverte/personnages/edmond-albius. Accessed August 25, 2010.

Root, Waverley. *Food*. New York: Simon & Schuster, 1980.

Schwarcz, Joe. *An Apple a Day: The Myths, Misconceptions and Truths about the Foods We Eat*. Toronto: Harper Perennial, 2007.

Sim, Alison. *Food and Feast in Tudor England*. Stroud, UK: Sutton Publishing, 1997.

Standage, Tom. *An Edible History of Humanity*. London: Atlantic Books, 2009.

Sun-Maid Growers of California. "History of Raisins and Dried Fruit." Available from: www.sun-maid.com/en/healthyliving/history_of_raisins_and_dried_fruit.html. Accessed August 30, 2010.

Clove in her new shoes

Swinnerton, Jo, ed. *The Cook's Pocket Companion*. London: Pavilion Books, 2004.

Vogel, Mark R. "A-Maize-ing I," August 6, 2008. Available from: www.foodreference.com/html/art-corn-history.html. Accessed July 20, 2010.

Wilson, Bee. *Swindled: From Poison Sweets to Counterfeit Coffee—The Dark History of the Food Cheats*. London: John Murray, 2008.

Wilson, Hilary. *Egyptian Food and Drink*. Princes Risborough, UK: Shire Publications, 2001.

Wood, Michael. *In Search of the First Civilizations*. London: BBC Books, 1992, 2005.

Zinczenko, David, and Matt Goulding. *Cook This, Not That!* New York: Rodale, 2010.

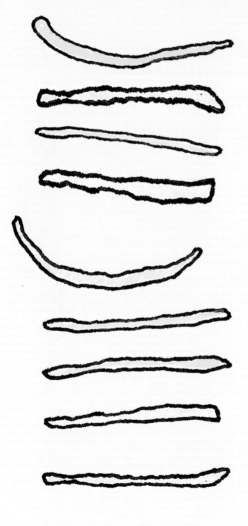

INDEX

Acknowledgments

A lot of people helped me with ideas and information for this book. My thanks to Tim, Susan, and Ika, who told me about foods around the world. I'm sorry that much of the material was left on the cutting room floor, but your information inspired me. Thanks also to researchers Louise Rolingher of the University of Alberta and Will Valley of the University of British Columbia, who reviewed the manuscript at various stages. And, most of all, thanks to my husband, Alan Daley, who enjoyed the research just as much as I did and who dished up lovely suppers to sustain me while I wrote.

—C.E.

Image Credits

Claire Eamer lives in the Yukon, in northern Canada, where she makes her living as a writer. She likes books, birds, science, history, traveling, and stories about magic. When she was a kid, she survived (to her mother's distress) on peanut butter and honey sandwiches and chocolate milk. Since then, she has tried a few more foods, and she likes almost all of them.

Sa Boothroyd, artist and tea maker, lives in the coastal village of Gibsons, in British Columbia, Canada, with her partner and two daughters. She likes to swim and bike for sanity, a quality that is not very evident in her drawings. Sa is intensely loyal to the foods she likes. When her favorite cereal went on sale, she bought 37 boxes— every last one in the store. She also enjoys scones and frozen toast.